Piranhas

By Susan Grossman

DILLON PRESS
New York

Acknowledgments

Much of this book is based on the research of Dr. Leo G. Nico, Dr. Ivan Sazima, and Dr. K. O. Winemiller. My sincerest thanks to Dr. Nico for his time, encouragement, and information.

Photo Credits

Photo research by Debbie Needleman
Cover courtesy of The Wildlife Collection/Jack Swenson
Back cover courtesy of the Audubon Institute/Mike De Mocker, provided by the Aquarium of the Americas, New Orleans

Audubon Institute/Mike De Mocker: frontispiece; John G. Shedd Aquarium/Edward G. Lines, Jr.: title page, 10; Dr. Leo G. Nico: 14, 17, 18, 20, 25, 27, 29, 31, 32, 36-37, 39, 42, 47, 49, 52, 53; Dr. Donald C. Taphorn: 22; Photo/Nats-Charles Steinmetz, Jr.: 44

Book design by Carol Matsuyama

Library of Congress Cataloging-in-Publication Data

Grossman, Susan M.
    Piranhas / by Susan Grossman. — 1st ed.
        p. cm. — (Remarkable animals)
    Includes index.
    Summary: Describes the physical characteristics, habitat, and life cycle of piranhas, and explains that their scary reputation may be exaggerated.
    ISBN 0-87518-593-2   0-382-39482-8 (pbk.)
    1. Piranhas—Juvenile literature. [1. Piranhas.] I. Title. II. Series: Remarkable animals series.
QL638.S483G76 1994
597'.52—dc   93-1772

Dillon Press   Maxwell Macmillan Canada, Inc.
Macmillan Publishing Company   1200 Eglinton Avenue East
866 Third Avenue   Suite 200
New York, NY 10022   Don Mills, Ontario M3C 3N1

Macmillan Publishing Company is part of the Maxwell Communication Group of Companies.
First edition
Printed in the United States of America
10 9 8 7 6 5 4 3 2

Contents

Facts about the Piranha

Scientific Names: Scientists used to lump all piranhas under the name *Serrasalmus*. Now scientists think there are at least four different groups of piranhas: *Serrasalmus, Pygocentrus, Pygopristis,* and *Pristobrycon*. Of these groups, scientists have identified some 30 different piranha species.

Description:

Size: From 8 inches (20 centimeters) to 2 feet (60 centimeters) long; most species a little over or under a foot (30 centimeters)

Physical Features: All piranhas have a single row of sharp, triangular-shaped teeth in both jaws; plate-shaped body, adipose fin; lower jaw sticks out farther than upper jaw. Some have heavy bodies with blunt, bulldog snout; others have longer body and sharp snout. They can see and hear well.

Color: Wide range of colors and black markings. All young piranhas have a silvery body. Adult piranhas are usually more colorful, often with bright red or orange bellies and throats—sometimes with yellow markings.

Distinctive Habits: Piranhas are active mostly during the day. Large piranhas may also hunt into the evening and early night, or before dawn. They may hunt in groups or alone. Many piranhas are social fish but sometimes bite one another and may eat another wounded piranha. Also, different species may prey on one another.

Some piranhas have very organized hunting behavior. They are not likely to attack a large healthy animal or human. In aquariums, they are not very aggressive unless they are hungry or overcrowded.

Food: Varied. All piranhas eat whole fish or pieces of flesh, but a few piranhas prefer to eat seeds or fruits. Young piranhas and some adults frequently eat pieces of fish fins and tails. Many piranhas are scavengers and eat dead flesh. Piranhas will also eat insects, shrimp, and fish scales. They will occasionally eat birds, rodents, and reptiles. Sometimes they will bite the toes and tail tips of swimming animals.

Reproduction: Scientists know very little about the reproduction of piranhas in the wild. Most piranhas in the wild breed at the beginning of the rainy season; females probably attach eggs to floating water plants and may make nests. Piranhas in aquariums are known to guard their eggs and their newly hatched young. Young piranhas hide and hunt among the roots and leaves of water plants. Piranhas are sexually mature, or can reproduce, after about one year. Older adult piranhas change color during the breeding season.

Life Span: Several years; some may live as long as five years or more.

Range of the Piranhas

Piranhas live in the area shaded in green

Range: Piranhas are freshwater tropical fish. They are only native to South America. Piranhas range from Venezuela south to the northern part of Argentina. They are found in all the major rivers that flow to the Atlantic Ocean, including the Amazon, Orinoco, Essequibo, La Plata, and São Francisco rivers.

Habitat: Piranhas are lowland fish that live in big rivers, small streams, and lagoons, as well as natural and man-made ponds, lakes, and reservoirs. They live in waters in both tropical forests and tropical savannas, or grasslands.

Only a few of the many kinds of piranhas are able to seriously injure a large animal. This Whimple piranha has weak jaws and lives on a diet of scales.

Chapter 1

A
Mysterious Fish

When you think of a piranha, you probably picture a fierce South American fish with razor-sharp, saw-like teeth. You might think of a river boiling with swarms of hungry fish, stripping an animal to bones in minutes. You probably wouldn't want to come face-to-face with a piranha.

But if you did, it's likely that the piranha would look you over, decide that you weren't good to eat, and swim away. That has been the experience of scientists who have snorkeled in rivers and lagoons where these fish live. The truth is that only a few of the many **species***, or kinds, of piranhas would be able to seriously harm a large animal.

* Words in **bold type** are explained in the glossary at the end of this book.

Even these would rather eat small fish, shrimp, tiny **crustaceans,** insects, the flesh of dead animals, and even fruit, seeds, and pieces of plants. Some piranhas prefer a diet of fins or scales from other fish. A few piranhas eat mostly vegetables.

Until recently, few scientists studied the behavior of piranhas in the wild, so very little is known about these mysterious fish that live in fresh water (water that is not salty) throughout most of South America. **Biologists** are just beginning to discover what piranhas do for a living.

An Important Fish

Piranhas have always affected the lives of the people who live near fresh water in South America. The presence of piranhas determines when and where people go into water and influences their choice of fishing methods. The fish are a large part of many people's diets, and piranha jaws are used as tools. In fact, piranhas have such an influence on the lives of South Americans who live near fresh water that many places are named after the fish. In 1899, a geographer named Moreira Pinto found 24 towns, rivers, mountains, and other areas called Piranha or Piranhas.

The name *piranha* comes from the South American Indian language Tupi-Guarani. *Piranha* is also what people along the Amazon River call scissors. The instrument was named for the fish, not the other way around. Long before scissors were invented, Indians in Guyana and the Amazon region used the jaws of the piranha as a cutting tool. Piranha jaws are still used as tools by some of the people who live along the waters of South America.

There are many other names for piranhas used by the people of South America. In southeastern Brazil, piranhas are often called *pirayas*. In Bolivia and Paraguay, the most common, dangerous piranha is called *palometa*, which means "little dove." In Venezuela, most piranhas are called *caribe*, after a warlike tribe of Indians. *Caribe* also means "cannibal."

Fish Stories

Most people outside South America first learned about piranhas in 1914 from Theodore Roosevelt, a former president of the United States. When he came back from his Amazon travels, he told terrifying stories about the fish. One story he told was about a soldier in Brazil who fell off his horse into the river and was eaten so completely that only his bones were left! It is probably true that the travelers found the soldier's skeleton, but it is most likely that he drowned and was later eaten by the many **aquatic** animals, including piranhas, that eat dead flesh.

How Dangerous Are They?

Not all scientists who study piranhas agree on how dangerous they are to people. There is no proof that a person has ever been killed by piranhas. In fact, most piranha bites occur when someone pulls a piranha out of the water and accidentally gets into its way as the fish throws itself around, snapping. Many fishermen have lost fingers and toes in this way.

Native American boys fishing for piranhas. The fish are an important source of protein, and the piranhas' jaws make excellent cutting tools.

On the other hand, there's no way of proving that piranhas have never killed a human. Although all piranhas have sharp teeth and strong jaws, several species are considered the most dangerous—or at least the most frightening. These include the red-bellied piranhas, the black piranhas, the pirayas of the São Francisco River in Brazil, and a species found in the Paraguay River. Besides having razor-sharp teeth that they use to clip bites of meat off **prey,** these are all big piranhas. Many animals in South American jungles lose toes and tail tips to the fish. Some, like the big black piranha, can bite through a man's wrist. So a group of these piranhas would certainly be able to hurt or kill a person.

Most scientists agree that piranhas could be dangerous under certain conditions. Piranhas get more aggressive—more likely to bite and fight—when they are crowded. This can happen at some times of the year when the water starts to dry out and the fish are pushed into smaller and smaller areas.

It could be dangerous to wade into a crowd of

Red-bellied piranhas, one of the more dangerous kinds of piranhas

piranhas that are eating, or feeding, because they could easily bite you by accident. Even though South Americans often go swimming in water where piranhas live, they don't go into water near slaughterhouses, where waste blood, bones, and meat are found. In those places, the groups of excited fish that gather to feed on the meat scraps are considered dangerous. There is a tree called the piranha

The red eye and strong jaws of the black piranha

tree that becomes covered with caterpillars once a year. Large groups of piranhas and other fish gather under this tree, waiting for the insects to fall. You would probably not want to take a walk along the shore under these trees, because the piranhas are ready to eat anything that falls into the water!

Piranhas, like some of their relatives, seem to be attracted to splashing. This is not surprising, because piranhas may take bites out of a wounded animal that falls into the water. When they hear splashing, they probably come to find out if it's being caused by an injured animal or just a fallen branch. But if the animal doesn't look as if it's hurt, they usually go away.

A Poor Pet

It is illegal to keep piranhas in some states in the United States. It is feared that released or escaped fish could make a home in southern waterways, like those of Florida or Louisiana. In fact, piranhas do not make especially good pets. People who own

them say that they are shy. But somehow a few piranhas still find their way into home aquariums. If you have a piranha, it is not a good idea to put your fingers in or near the water. The fish might mistake them for food and bite them. In general, though, piranhas in aquariums are not very aggressive unless they are crowded or underfed.

South Americans often swim and bathe in waters where piranhas live.

These are skulls of piranhas that have recently died. The piranha's distant ancestors date back some 100 million years.

22

Chapter 2

A Closer Look

The Piranha's Ancestors

About 100 million years ago, the ancestors of the piranha appeared. They showed up in a freshwater lake on a continent that is now Africa and South America. The piranha's ancestors had one feature that distinguished them from earlier fish: a chain of small bones called **Weber's ossicles.** They allowed the fish to hear better, especially high-pitched sounds. Weber's ossicles act like the bones in your middle ear, which conduct vibrations from the eardrum to the inner ear. In the fish, they are the first four vertebrae of the backbone.

Scientists **classify** fish that have Weber's ossicles as ostariophysans. They date their appearance at about 100 million years ago because the first **fossils** of fish having this new feature date from that time. Equipped with sharper hearing, ostariophysans were very successful. They **evolved** into many different groups of freshwater fish. One of the first was the characoids. Piranhas are characoids, so they were among the first fish to have the advantages of good hearing. They could find food more easily and were better able to escape **predators** than other kinds of fish.

Besides their Weber's ossicles, all characoids have other things in common. Most have a fleshy little fin, called an **adipose fin,** on their back close to the tail, and most of them have scales. Nearly all characoids have teeth.

When the continents of Africa and South America separated, the characoid fish evolved into different types on both sides of the Atlantic Ocean. In South America, they were especially free to expand because they had little competition: There were few other fish that ate the same food, and if they did, they were not as good at finding it or catching it.

24

This silver dollar is a cousin of the piranha, part of the subfamily Serrasalminae.

As a result, about 80 percent of the 1,200 or so known species of characoids live in South America. There are probably as many species that haven't been discovered yet!

Scientists classify characoid fish further, into smaller groups. Piranhas are part of the family Characidae and the subfamily Serrasalminae, which means "**serrated** salmon." The subfamily Serrasalminae includes all the piranhas and their relatives, such as the pacus and silver dollars. Scientists think there are at least 30 different piranha species.

Different Fish, Different Habits

Most piranhas have a body shaped like a round dinner plate, with spines on the belly and many small scales. Many also have blunt noses and lower jaws that stick out farther than their upper jaws, making them look a little like bulldogs. The largest piranhas grow to be about 2 feet (about 60 centimeters) long. One of these lives in the São Francisco River in northeastern Brazil. You may think it lucky that this big hunter lives in only one river—but since that river is nearly 2,000 miles (3,200 kilometers) long, the piranha's range still covers a great deal of territory. Most other piranhas are a little over or a little under 1 foot (about 30 centimeters) long. There are many species of smaller piranhas whose average size is between 8 and 12 inches (20 and 30 centimeters).

All piranhas have a single row of teeth in each jaw, and each tooth is shaped like a triangle. The upper and lower teeth slide against one another to shear off pieces of food—working like a powerful pair of scissors. If a piranha loses a tooth on one side

The strong jaws of a piranha. The sharp teeth in each jaw slide against one another to slice off pieces of food like a pair of scissors.

of its jaw, it must grow an entirely new set on that side. Piranhas don't chew—once they bite out a chunk of food, they swallow it whole.

Even though all piranhas have very similar types of teeth, different kinds of piranhas often use their teeth for different purposes. Not all piranhas prefer to eat whole fish or take bites out of fishes' bodies. Young piranhas and adults of some species

27

frequently clip out pieces of other fishes' fins and tails. Most piranhas will also bite off and swallow fish scales. Piranhas, especially young ones, will eat insects and small crustaceans. Adult piranhas will occasionally eat birds, rodents and other mammals, reptiles, and frogs. They will sometimes bite toes and tail tips of swimming animals also.

Only a few species of piranhas are able to seriously injure a large live animal or human. These include the red-bellied piranhas that most people think of when they hear the word *piranha*. They live in the Amazon Basin and in the Orinoco River, which flows through Venezuela and borders Colombia. Red-bellied piranhas grow to more than 14 inches (37 centimeters) long. Red-bellies live mostly in lagoons. One scientist said they were the most beautiful freshwater fish, with an olive green or brown face, a gold or silver back, a black tail, and red everywhere else. Black piranhas have powerful jaws, strong enough to bite through wood. Their eyes are red. Black piranhas are most

Exposing the razor-sharp teeth of *Pygocentrus caribe*—the "cannibal" from Venezuela

common in streams of the Amazon and the Orinoco.

Piranha Relatives

Pacus look like piranhas but have two rows of teeth in the upper jaw. Some teeth are shaped like **molars,** the large, flat teeth you chew with. Pacus use their molarlike teeth to grind fruit, nuts, and leaves. Pacus also have sharp, **incisor**-like teeth and will eat insects, small shellfish, and fish. Some pacus grow very large, up to 3 feet (90 centimeters) long, and are important as food to people of the Amazon Basin. Some young pacus are colorful and make good aquarium fish. However, people who own pacus say that they will kill and eat other fish when they grow larger and start feeling cramped for space.

Surprising Diets

Until very recently, scientists thought that all piranhas ate only fish and meat. They called them carnivores—meat eaters. But scientists have discovered that some piranhas are more vegetarian than flesh

Missing part of its tail, this tropical fish has fallen prey to a fin-eating piranha.

eaters—they prefer to eat seeds and fruits that fall into the water. Piranha teeth work equally well in biting out a piece of hard seed as they do in clipping out a piece of flesh. Even the more carnivorous piranhas will eat fruits and seeds at certain times of the year when such foods are more plentiful than fish. They'll also bite at pieces of aquatic plants.

Most piranhas are also **scavengers**—they eat the flesh of dead animals and people. It's likely that this habit contributed to the piranha's reputation for being a "man-eater"—when a skeleton is pulled out of the water, it's hard to tell how the person died.

Chapter 3

Piranhas at Home

Picture pushing a block of clay against a wall. The clay next to the wall would be crunched upward. That is basically how the Andes mountain chain was formed on the western coast of South America some 70 million years ago. Think again of the clay. The area behind where it was pushed up would buckle downward. That corresponds to the formation of the Amazon Basin, a depression in the earth that runs the length of South America east of the Andes. After the mountains formed, the basin became a huge lake. Later the great lake drained into the Atlantic Ocean. It left behind a thick, rich lake bed that is now a grass- and forest-covered plain with many thousands of rivers and lakes.

This huge Amazon Basin, with its lush plant

One of the many fresh waterways in the lush Amazon Basin, where piranhas make their home life and many bodies of fresh water, is the biggest basin in the world and home to a vast number of fish species, including the piranhas. Piranhas are found in much of South America—but nowhere else in the world, at least not naturally. The fish range from Venezuela south to the northern part of Argentina. They are found in all the major South American rivers that flow to the Atlantic Ocean, including the Amazon, Orinoco, Essequibo, La Plata, and São Francisco. Piranhas are lowland fish that live in both big rivers and small streams. They also inhabit lagoons, ponds, lakes, and reservoirs. They live in fresh waters in both tropical forests and tropical savannas, or grasslands. Piranhas do not live in mountain streams or lakes, probably because the water is much too cold and flows too swiftly to allow the fish to catch what little food there is in such places.

South America's climate can vary greatly from one region to another, from the hot deserts of Chile to the cold peaks of the Andes. Since the continent crosses the equator, most of South America is warm most of the time. Rather than having a true summer or winter, the **tropics** have a rainy season and a dry season. And the piranha's world is quite different from one season to another.

The heavy rains start very suddenly and slowly taper off months later. Some areas that are flat and grassy in the dry season become covered with water in the wet season. These **floodplains** are home to a huge number of animals—ducks, storks, herons, turtles, crocodiles, snakes, and capybaras (the biggest rodents—more than 4 feet [1.2 meters] long). And of course, there are lots of fish—catfish, stingrays, electric eels, and many more, including piranhas and pacus.

Some animals prey upon piranhas. Many fish, birds, and other animals that live in or near water eat small or young piranhas. The large piranhas have fewer predators, but even they can make a meal for wading birds, giant otters, river dolphins, large catfish, and caimans (South and

Herons, ibis, and egrets gather on a floodplain. While they often prey on piranhas, these waterbirds are sometimes attacked and eaten by the sharp-toothed fish.

Central American alligators)—as well as for humans.

During the rainy season, South American rain forests in lowland areas often flood, creating swamps. These areas, called flooded forests, are underwater up to ten months of the year, and the plants have all kinds of special features that allow them to survive being underwater for so long. After the rain stops, the flooded areas gradually dry and the water level of rivers, streams, lagoons, and water holes drops, crowding the fish into smaller and smaller areas.

Wary Neighbors

In almost any place where there is one kind of piranha, there will be several other species, too. Usually, three or more species of piranhas can be found in the same area. Different kinds of piranhas may bite at one another.

Piranhas are usually most active during the day. Different species, though, sometimes hunt at different times. This may keep the several sorts of

A piranha predator, this wide-mouthed catfish is able to swallow piranhas whole.

piranhas in a body of water from competing for the same food at the same time. It may also prevent them from eating one another.

Even within the same species, piranhas of different ages may be active at different times. At night, younger, smaller fish tend to rest among the water plants, leaving the open waters to older and bigger fish. This prevents adult piranhas from making a meal of the young fish. By about 10:00 P.M., even the largest piranha has usually retired for the night.

Some kinds of piranhas gather in groups. Others swim alone. They may pick out an area and patrol it, checking it for food. At night or when they're resting, they hide among plants in the shallow water.

A Skilled Hunter

At first glance, it may seem that piranhas just swim around in a group, eating anything at any time. But in fact, piranhas use many different hunting methods. They may hide among plants or rocks, waiting for prey to come close. Then they rush out and capture or bite it. They might sneak up on their prey. They might even act as if they're not interested in a fish until they're close enough to reach it. Some piranhas that look like the fish they eat approach in disguise, behaving like one of their targets until they get close enough to grab a bite. Some kinds of piranhas, like the ones that eat scales, fins, and tails, are slimmer and faster than other

40

species, and they chase down other fish. Most piranhas, however, aren't fast enough to catch fish racing through open water.

Some piranhas behave like lions that hunt zebras or antelope. A scientist saw a group of scale-eating piranhas hunting a school of fish. One piranha rushed in and scattered the group of prey fish. Then each piranha picked out one fish to bite some scales from. Piranhas will also take advantage of the confusion when other hunting fish scatter a school.

Piranhas also scavenge, searching for bits of flesh and dead animals. Many aquatic animals such as catfish and crabs are scavengers, but when the piranhas come, they back away and let the piranhas eat.

Avoiding the Hunters

Some fish have evolved behaviors or features that lessen their chances of being attacked by piranhas. Fish that are preyed on by fin-eating piranhas may

Some tropical fish like this pike cichlid have a spot near the tail that looks like an eye. These false eyes provide protection against piranhas that nip fish tails.

hide their tails in plants. Some of these, such as the Oscar, have a circular mark near their tail that looks very much like an eye. This false eye probably confuses piranhas, and therefore they do not attack.

Some schools of fish have one fish keep watch while the rest eat. Sometimes prey fish fight back, or a group of them might rush toward a piranha and chase it away. Many other fish avoid piranhas by coming out only at night.

Most piranhas have some red coloring on their body. Many of the fish that piranhas eat also have red coloring. The red color might fool the piranha into thinking the other fish is one of its own kind and give the fish a chance to escape. Or the red color might make other fish avoid eating the red fish, mistaking it for a piranha. Scientists aren't entirely sure what the purpose of this particular **mimicry** is.

Lords of the Water

Piranhas are very important fish in the freshwater **ecosystem** of the Amazon Basin and throughout most of South America. Because they are such successful predators, their behavior affects the way other prey fish behave and perhaps even how they look. It's easy to see why piranhas are sometimes called "lords of the water."

A red-bellied piranha dressed in its "wedding finery." Usually silver and red, it has turned black with glittering flecks of gold.

Chapter 4

The Piranha's Year

The dry season is in full force on a floodplain in Venezuela. Since January, the sheets of water that covered the land have been drying, and by the beginning of April much of the water has evaporated. Fish are crowded into the small remaining pools. Many have died for lack of water and oxygen. But few of the fish in these pools are adult piranhas. Where are they?

No one knows for sure, but scientists think that the piranhas have **migrated** to deeper water downstream. They will return very soon after the rainy season starts, a month from now.

Wedding Finery

When the piranhas return, both male and female

adults will be wearing different colors than they do during the rest of the year, because they will be ready to **breed.** The Orinoco red-bellied piranha, usually silver and red, turns black with glittering purple or gold flecks. The black piranha turns even darker. Many colorful piranhas are more colorful and beautiful than usual. The female piranhas **spawn**, or lay eggs, during the rainy season.

Piranhas probably **court** each other, like their relatives the tetras do. Tetra males and females go through a set of paired movements, as though they were dancing together, before they spawn. It is likely that piranhas do something similar. Right now, scientists know very little about how wild piranhas breed. They are probably **sexually mature,** or old enough to reproduce, when they're about a year old.

Spawning

No one is really sure about the spawning habits of wild piranhas. In aquariums, some females just lay their eggs on the floor of the tank, but others have

Scientists have cut open this adult female piranha to examine her ovaries and small yellow eggs.

been seen readying a nest. These spend a great deal of time choosing a spot near water plants and then cleaning it with their fins. When the fish lay their eggs, the eggs stay stuck to the plants. Then the males swim near and deposit sperm on the eggs. In the wild, it may be that piranhas behave differently. No one is sure whether the fish also guard their nests or the newly hatched piranhas. Some scientists think they do, but very few people have actually seen them behaving this way.

Young Piranhas at Home

In the wild, the young piranhas hide among the stems and roots of the water plants. These plants cover the riverbank and form floating clumps on the surface of the water. The tiniest piranhas, less than 1 inch (about 2 centimeters) long, spend their entire time there. They swim slowly through the thick tangle of plants, looking for tiny crustaceans, **immature** insects, and aquatic worms. When the little piranhas are a bit bigger, they sometimes venture away from the plants to hunt small fish. They come back to rest and hide among the plants at night. The plants protect the little piranhas from larger piranhas and other predators, as well as from one another.

The plants may serve another purpose for the piranhas. The clumps of plants often break loose and

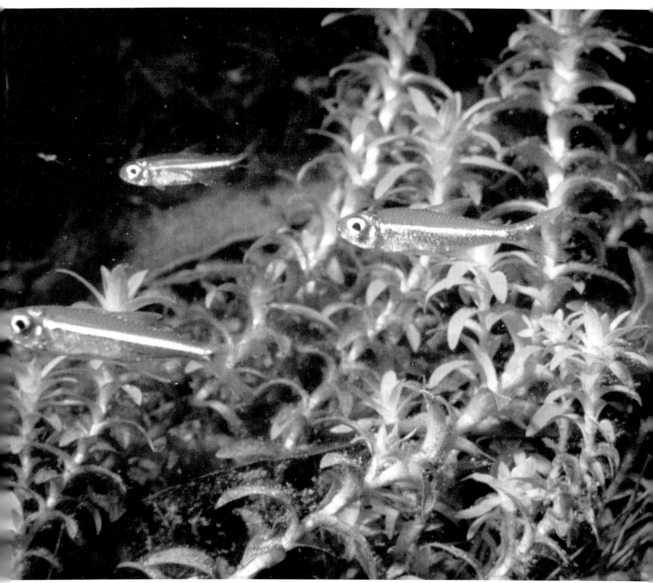

Young fish glide through clusters of water plants that protect them from predators.

float down the river. When the plants float away, tiny piranhas and other fish passengers go with them. Eventually the plants bump into something and stop moving, and the fish settle down in their new home. In this way, piranhas are distributed throughout the lowland waterways of South America. Some people think that a way to control piranhas where they are pests might be to destroy or move the plants instead of trying to kill the fish.

Piranhas and People

Piranhas have a frightening reputation, but people have been getting along with them and making use of them for thousands of years. Their jaws are still used as cutting tools and their teeth as razors by some of the rain forest people of South America.

Some groups of people use piranhas as undertakers. The Orinoco River floods its banks and turns the surrounding grasslands into floodplains. When the earth is underwater, dead people can't be buried. Instead, the bodies are left in the water. Within a few hours, only a skeleton is left. The skeleton is then retrieved, and the bones are dried, dyed, and decorated. When the land dries, the bones are finally buried. This may be another reason that one of the piranha's names is *caribe*—cannibal.

Piranhas are also an important food. In Brazil, fishermen bait "trotlines," fishing lines tied between two poles or trees in a lake. Each string has several hooks tied to it that hang just below the surface of the water. A fisherman sets out as many as 15 of these trotlines at a time. Some fishermen bait their hooks with shrimp and jiggle the poles. When the piranhas come to eat the shrimp, the fishermen lift them out of the water and club them on the head. If the fishermen threw the piranhas into the boat before they did that, the men could easily get bitten.

Many people consider piranhas pests and would like to get rid of them. Piranhas make fishing difficult. They eat fish that are caught in a net or on a pole. They destroy nets with their teeth, and sometimes

Piranhas are good to eat. Here, fish vendors sell their piranha catch in the marketplace of a South American city.

bite through fishhooks. People herding animals across rivers worry that parts of the animal that hang underwater might be bitten. And although few swimmers get bitten by piranhas, care must be taken around the fish. When hungry piranhas are crowded into a small area, it could be unsafe to be among them.

This big catfish was caught in an underwater net. Before the fishermen could retrieve it, piranhas took their share.

A Useful Fish

But in some ways, piranhas are actually friends of the fishing industry. Piranhas can't usually catch and kill healthy fish. It is often the slower, weaker, or diseased fish that they catch. In this way, they keep the fish population strong and stop fish **epidemics** from spreading. And because piranhas eat dead creatures,

53

they dispose of flesh that would otherwise poison the water.

You might not think that fish have anything to do with trees, but piranhas are friends of the forest, too. They are important in the **ecology** of the more than two million square miles (nearly five million square kilometers) of Amazon rain forest, the largest tropical rain forest in the world. Piranhas eat seeds that fall into the water and then swim away. They expel some of the seeds undamaged in their waste matter. If the seeds fall into a proper environment, they may sprout, spreading the forest.

Rain forests are very special environments. They are home to almost half of the species of plants and animals on earth. They are also home to some groups of people. Many useful products—some varieties of fruit, wood, fiber, and the drugs quinine and curare—are found nowhere else.

The tropical forests of the world are disappearing so quickly that the larger blocks of forest may be gone within 20 years. Trees are being cut down to make room for humans, their farm animals, their industries, and their homes. As a result, scientists are afraid that destroying the tropical forests will make the world an unfit place to live.

In some places, piranhas have been poisoned to get rid of them, but no one really knows what the long-term results of this action will be. Like the tropical forests they help to maintain, the piranhas are irreplaceable and unique.

Scientists are just beginning to discover facts about the behavior and life cycle of piranhas. The more that is known about them, the less people will fear these fascinating, mysterious fish.

Glossary

adipose fin (AD-uh-pose fin)—a small fleshy fin on a fish's back, close to the tail

aquatic (uh-KWAT-ik)—living in water

biologist (by-OL-uh-just)—scientist who studies living things

breed—to produce young

classify—to arrange living things into groups according to their relationships. One system puts all living things into five groups, called kingdoms: plants, animals, bacteria, fungi (FUN-jy), and Protista (one-celled living things). The kingdoms are divided into groups. Each group is smaller than the previous group: phylum, class, order, family, genus, and species. Each of these groups may be divided, as well.

court—to behave in a way that attracts another animal for the purpose of mating

crustacean (kruhs-TAY-shun)—an animal that has a hard shell and lives mostly in water. Lobsters, crabs, shrimp, and many tiny organisms such as water fleas and seed shrimp are crustaceans.

ecology (ih-KAHL-uh-jee)—the scientific study of the relationships between animals and plants and the surroundings in which they live

56

ecosystem (EH-ko-sis-tem)—a community consisting of plants, animals, and other natural features in which all members affect one another

epidemic (ep-uh-DEM-ik)—a disease that is spread among a large number of animals or plants

evolve (ee-VAHLV)—to change over time

floodplains (FLUD-playnz)—lowland areas bordering rivers that are covered with water during the rainy season

fossil (FAHS-al)—a piece of an animal or plant that has been preserved in the earth. A fossil can also be preserved in other materials, such as resin, amber, or tar, or be an impression left by an animal or plant.

immature (im-uh-CHUR)—not fully grown

incisor (in-SY-zuhr)—a sharp tooth, designed for cutting

migrate (MY-grate)—to move from one place to another for feeding or breeding

mimicry (MIM-ih-kree)—the practice of copying other animals, plants, or objects that are part of an animal's or plant's surroundings. Mimicry helps increase an animal's or plant's chances of survival.

molar (MOE-luhr)—teeth with a round or flat surface, designed for grinding food

predator (PRED-uh-tuhr)—an animal that hunts other animals

prey—animals that are hunted by other animals

scavenger (SKAV-uhn-juhr)—an animal that eats dead flesh or bits of food that it finds

serrated (suh-RATE-ed)—having a sawlike edge

sexually mature—old enough to produce young

spawning—the laying of eggs in large numbers by aquatic animals

species (SPEE-sheez)—a group of plants or animals that have common characteristics and share a common name

tropics—a region of the earth that is near the equator

Weber's ossicles (WEB-uhrz AHS-see-kuhlz)—a chain of small bones formed from the first four vertebrae of the backbone in certain fish. They allow the fish to hear high-pitched sounds.

Index

Susan M. Grossman has been filling her home with animals and her notebooks with observations on their behavior since she was a child in New York City. Her experience in zoological research and her graduate education in biopsychology have led her to believe that animals are worth knowing about, not for what they say about people but for what they say about themselves. She currently lives in Seattle, Washington.